Voices in the Garden

Voices in the Garden

Lucia Chiappara-Bennett

iUniverse LLC
Bloomington

VOICES IN THE GARDEN

iUniverse books may be ordered through booksellers or by contacting:

iUniverse LLC
1663 Liberty Drive
Bloomington, IN 47403
www.iuniverse.com
1-800-Authors (1-800-288-4677)

ISBN: 978-1-4917-1702-8 (sc)
ISBN: 978-1-4917-1703-5 (e)

Printed in the United States of America.

iUniverse rev. date: 11/26/2013

Contents

Introduction.. ix

A Whispering Queen...1
All I Wanted Was to Feel Loved...2
Beauty's Eyes 3
Bello..4
Bigger Hearts 5
Delusional...6
Demands...7
Dreams Turned Cold 8
Fear...9
Flawless...10
Good-Bye..11
Grace 12
He Didn't Say Hello 13
I Don't Mind 14
I Found Love 15
I Remember!...16
I Sing...17
If I Could Find a Miracle..18
If I Dream..19
I'm Looking.. 20
Important Love..21
In Trouble 22
Inside the Frame... 23

It Doesn't Matter 24
It Wasn't My Fault.. 25
It's Hard to Let Go.. 26
Lady Love Bug 27
Listening for My Soul 28
Looking for That Sound 29
Looking Inside Yourself 30
Looks...31
Milan.. 32
Months...33
My Life, My Dreams 34
My Mother's Presence... 35
No Touching 36
One-Night Stand 37
Open Your Mind 38
Overwhelming Hearts... 39
Picture on the Wall 40
Poets' Expectations 41
Pure Lust.. 42
Reach for a Carrie 43
Realization.. 44
Remorse 45
Sabrina 46
Since When 47
Singing a Different Tune 48
Someone Is Watching 49
Sophisticate 50
Sound 51
Standards..52
Such Concerns and Such Liberation....................................53
Surprise.. 54
The Ghost 55
The Harvest 56

The Queen 57

There's No Time 58

This Kind.. 59

Timid.. 60

Decline...61

Insecure 62

Untitled.. 63

Vivid Blackmail.. 64

With or Without a Kiss 65

Within Yourself.. 66

You Don't Know What I Want 67

You Don't Need to Know 68

You're Not Happy... 69

About the Book... 71

About the Author 73

Introduction

When I first had the heart to write, I knew I had something that I could believe in. I felt inspired by what I saw and how I felt. I had experiences based on my perceptions and disappointments. But when I hooked on to my true passion for poetry, it was hard to turn my back on how I felt toward others and my dreams. I felt this was something that needed to be told. Thanks to everyone who gave me that experience. My family has clearly reflected on my independence and patience. They get along well with my abilities. I had to grow a lot in order to live the kind of life I wanted, leeching myself on others and building inspiration along the way. My elementary school teacher provided strong growth and helped me learn the meaning of writing poetry. She fulfilled her dedication and inspiration until the end. I dedicate my love and inspiration to my family.

A Whispering Queen

She cried and cried
Until she whispered to her lover, night.
As the queen ran alone,
Never to be seen again,
The whispering queen laid her head down with sadness,
Wanting to end her life,
Yet she came close to making it alive.
Each moment got darker and colder
Waiting for the night to arrive,
But he never showed his long, narrow face.
She returned her love to the tower of Emerdello.

All I Wanted Was to Feel Loved

I know what love is and how love feels,
But sharing the same dreams is just like this.
All I wanted was to share it with you.
Soon you started to change your mind.
Change makes it hard to keep love the same.
You feel the fears as I try to close,
As you blame the values of my peers
And how I look,
As you started to sneer,
As nothing was the same, to try to find the game we play.
You gave up looking and started to demand, to turn away.
All I wanted was to feel loved,
And I'm still not good enough for your true love.

Beauty's Eyes

All heaven's doors opened.
As I desire to fly,
I waved good-bye.
As when the beauty can't be ignored,
I came back.
The pink nose gently lies beneath its ocean breeze.
Soon heaven's doors didn't mind
To offer an open hand,
To lie, preaching gently,
As the pink nose bloomed,
Judging as they were gazing.
Now they said, "We are steam with your kindliness.
Now let us go."
Impatience lip had care deeply into prayers.
As they kissed and smiled
When reassuring them to fall in love.

Bello

Ciao, Come sta?
Bello romantico
Noi parleremo
With your golden brown eyes
And long brown hair—
Such handsome and masculine features—
Come with me and you'll see.
Nothing will stop us now.
Not a soul will bring us misery,
But love will give us joy and happiness!

Bigger Hearts

I miss you, and you miss me.
I love you, and you love me.
We don't see each other,
But we are here until the end.
No matter where or no matter how,
Bigger hearts and bigger love will be together forever!

Delusional

I envision you as delusional,
Judging the lust of my sins,
Demanding to cloister my soul,
Fear, in spite of my sins,
Lingering. You are false to me,
Fearing your knowledge in spite of me,
Delusional, maybe, within your deliberation
And knowing who you really are.

Demands

I feel threatened by your motives
As your demands leave emotions.
The reason for the immensity of the crisis—
My remains left splintered in frustration.
As I glance with no equal sense of respect,
I reserve myself against men,
The smell of maintaining aroma
As you failed to experience your demands.
I grow outside as I interact with the fear of emptiness,
Making change to achieve your resolving discoveries.
Pushing me away and juggling to crisis,
You undermine the concepts of hating me,
But hating becomes so fundamental to a dangerous soul
As you emerge, difficult boundaries.

Dreams Turned Cold

It wasn't me, and it wasn't you,
But I felt that nothing was true.
My dreams didn't last;
They didn't last too long.
I'm writing this to make you see
That my love didn't belong to you.
He didn't love me.
He didn't love you.
Dreams turned cold
Like it was that day.
It wasn't me, and it wasn't you,
But I felt that nothing was true.
Soon we leave—
That nothing was true.

Fear

I fear how high I jumped or climbed
As I fear how high I reached for the sky.
I live every minute
As I see it from the ground.
My heart falls, and I still fear the sound.
No one should see
And no one should hear,
But I fear how high I see tonight.

Flawless

When the moment came, I felt my love.
I had flirted with emotion and desire to see
If I would respond to your love.
I felt emotion enough, but not loud enough,
To achieve the most desire.
I reach, ignored and scared
That you still have concerns.
I am right here
Waiting, flawless but scared.
There wasn't any time,
Standing in the dark
As I watched the unexpected,
As I responded loud enough to you.

Good-Bye

We waited for our time
As our memories were left behind
To say good-bye to all the things
As we were leading our lives
That left our feelings inside
When we laughed, prayed, or cried!
To all the memories that we left behind
When everything was too late to say good-bye!

Grace

I heard your soul
Surrounding the sorrows with your prayers
As I touched the warmth of your affection,
A graceful prayer for each above
That showed the words of your compassion,
My love, my faith, and my grace!
That surrendered the peace upon the land.

He Didn't Say Hello . . .

I arrived raising my hand,
Rising to ring the bell,
But scattering my fears
As I spread my whispering soul
That love was the reason for my words.
As I arrived, as I glanced from afar,
As I posed my lips
And I spun around to kiss,
Raising my heart without a tear,
As I glanced without a word of hello,
I knew as I heard,
"You're arrogant and loud"—
Indeed I felt a victim of love,
A threat of betrayal
As he slammed the door without saying hello!

I Don't Mind

I don't mind if you dance all night.
I don't mind if you sing all night.
As I dream, I dream to shine.
I know I watch you from the start.
I don't sleep.
I don't eat.
But I smell food from afar;
I hunt for love to stay alive.
I don't mind if you dance all night.
I don't mind if you sing all night.
But I know I dream to shine.

I Found Love

I have found love:
It was underneath all the charm,
And it gave me strength
But one who ravages one's love—
They'll emerge through my soul
Without dragging its love and emptiness
As far as they can go.
But I keep my love hidden
Underneath all my sins and soul.
I use my strength and my charm
Without fear and emptiness inside
As far as they can go!

I Remember!

I see a vision of disagreements.
I remember . . .
I see you treat love poorly
As I saw you feeling unhappy
And too much resistance.
I learned to trade feelings,
Trying hard to avoid emotions
When love was too negative
But was disappointed
That love was too short.
Focus to reunite you and the past.
But when I look at the truth
And I see the positive,
I see regrets,
But I keep it real,
And lost cost encourages me to give up the truth.

I Sing

I sing in the night.
I sing in the day.
I sing in the rain.
I feel no pain
For what I sing.
I feel so gay
When I sing
I sing until May.

If I Could Find a Miracle

If I could find a miracle,
I would change my ways.
Everyone would love to have me closer
If I could find a miracle.
I would give answers to everything
And feel pleasant and kind to everyone around.
If I could find a miracle,
I would walk to every land around me,
Showing you that there is more to life to love and cherish.
If I could find a miracle,
There wouldn't be any more hate and killing
But a wisdom of love and kindness.
If I could find a miracle,
There would be fewer painful memories,
And everyone would be graceful.

If I Dream

You feel unsatisfied by fulfilling my dreams
As if you shatter my dreams of deliverance,
Your dreams of things that are not true.
But when I dream of reserve and comfort
As if I put my love too close to effort
And I see my dreams with love and closure,
As my remains are left to find fulfillment,
You ignore the loss of freedom and effort.

I'm Looking

I'm looking for the universe
As I choose to walk alone.
I use my long legs;
Who can see or watch me pass?
I can choose to use the empire,
But they own my name.
Everything around me is bigger and taller,
But I feel no shame and smaller.
I couldn't speak to anyone,
But who would listen to my words?
I'm looking for the universe
As I choose to walk alone.

Important Love

Often love can be defined;
General words are worth a try.
Important love can be abused.
Where is our pride?
But deep inside, love is emotion
Left free in never-ending tales of lies
Like the wonders of compassion and perfection
As I touch the soft depths of illusion
That often have carried me to valuable conclusions.

In Trouble

I feel I'm in trouble
As I increase my love.
For the tears of my love
I'm looking for healing,
But something to procrastinate
Only brought me more trouble
As I posed my thoughts,
As I endearment of trust
That persist obedient soul
When only brought me more trouble.

Inside the Frame

I'm inside the frame,
Surrounded by the sound of the voice
Whispering the most gentle touch,
The face that stares among the clouds,
Looking back at me,
Feeling the emotions.
Each moment I lay among the soft touch,
My movement inside myself had a single flare,
Looking, looking as I felt the kiss of a touch.

It Doesn't Matter . . .

It doesn't matter what I say.
It doesn't matter what I do.
I'm allowed to feel my desire.
When I'm feeling sad or feeling mad,
I consider feeling compassion,
But someone will always interfere.
It doesn't matter if someone would
have followed my desires;
I run and hide.
You can find me underneath a broken tree.
You can find me underneath a leaf.
There's nothing to see inside me.
All I wanted was to feel inspired.
I'm not careless,
But I feel contrary inside.

It Wasn't My Fault

It wasn't my fault
When the star flew over.
It wasn't my fault
When the car tipped over.
It wasn't my fault
When the jar fell over.
It wasn't my fault
When the garbage tipped over.
It wasn't my fault
When the game was over.
It wasn't my fault
When I had nothing left over.
Welcome over!

It's Hard to Let Go

My heart wants you to know
That you knew what was mine.
It's hard to let it go,
But now it's hard to fulfill my happiness,
Trying to hide the insults and crime.
You made me feel like a fool
When you took something that was so cruel.
I linger into the night
As I try to find my freedom.
I still think about what was mine.
It's hard to let it go.

Lady Love Bug

Oh, lady love bug!
Oh, lady love bug!
How I wonder where you are.
I see you in the daytime.
I can't find you in the spring.
I'm searching for you up and down,
All around.
Did you fly up to the sky? No!
Did you land on the ground? No!
Are you in the tree?
Behind the tree?
On the leaves?
On the ground?
Oh, lady love bug!
Oh, lady love bug!
Where are you?
There you are—
I found you landing on my nose.

Listening for My Soul

When I listen,
I listen to the way it sounds,
I listen with my heart,
I listen with my soul.
The way it sounds is too good to be true.
Keeping what influence, my love,
I closely respond to you.

Looking for That Sound

I walked far for so long
Like I was about to vanish.
I kept looking around, and
I walked into the darkness.
Wondering what to do,
No color or sound
Under my feet, I stood on ground.
And I could feel that there was balance,
So I started walking,
And I waited for something to hit me.
But nothing hurt me!
So I stopped and closed my eyes
Until I heard a sound.
I opened my eyes, and then
I could see roses all around.

Looking Inside Yourself

You don't know how it feels,
Looking inside yourself,
When something feels lonely and scared.
You don't know how it feels,
Thinking of how to spare
When something feels lonely and scared.
You don't know what to expect
After all the memories disappear.
You don't know howit feels,
Looking inside yourself,
When our dreams pass us by
Under all these feelings, wounded
When looking deep inside yourself.
But all these feelings wash away
Without having any fear.
You don't know how it feels,
Looking inside yourself,
When something feels lonely and scared;
You don't know how it feels
As if you think of how to spare.

Looks

Looks have nothing to do with how we feel
When anger makes everyone inside look so real.
You have seen within your fears,
Melting your measure of lies.
Believe in what was once so fine—
Is what we learn to open our minds
When we open our eyes to love?
But you'll never see the right or wrong,
Refusing to stand so high and tall.
Look around before you sing this song
As if we live to blame the values on the wall.

Milan

There was a time,
There was a place,
When I spoke of you.
You made things so open, love,
But to far more loved
You tormented me with harsh and dangerous words.
You were wroth with me;
That scared me.
Now how can I stop?
Stop thinking of how to say no!
I read your unopened letters
That surrendered your love to Maria.
How could you?
How could you make me feel so low?
You allowed yourself to feel so dangerous.

Milan Milan **Milan**

Months

I look at the months
And nowhere to be found.
I traveled days and nights
As nowhere to be seen.
I had spoken too soon
When sneers end with cold winter months
And cold winter days.
As thoughts of loneliness close in to be near,
Its coldness overlaps slightly on my skin
Strips, layers of months and endless fears,
As I see changes in clear spring
Speaking in the winds of your hot, sunny days
Yet I can smell, and fresh coldness remains the same.

My Life, My Dreams

I achieved time
And again my dreams
As I expect change
That's worth my time.
I feel satisfied when you're on my side,
But there was interference.
That dream achieved,
And I gather altitude
As if I had achieved my life.

My Mother's Presence

I twinkled rapidly into my thoughts
Sitting in the house of the Lord;
I looked above as I felt my mother's presence.
The music softly restored her beauty;
I watched as I surrendered my sins.
Nearly my love had ever seen
I threw my expressions into sensitivity and emotion.
As she pointed out her faith and love,
She corrupted her love in seeing my daughter and me.
Unable myself to move or to swallow,
I lay to rest my sins as I dream of the imaginative soul
And comfort myself that she is still watching over us.

No Touching

One love can keep us alive;
That can pass us by—
I grew to believe that
When it had torn us apart—
Torn by what goes around.
When I felt that love didn't belong,
I couldn't reach to survive.
That love was no longer for the stars
And no touching was allowed.

One-Night Stand

I gush through life with innocents,
Looking above the noisy mentors
As if you were to lie upon the whispering soul.
Only looking for a one-night stand!
I had spent my lust upon spirited minds.
I had found nothing but him
Wishing for the hand of the innocent lady,
Refusing the gentle touch and glory!

Open Your Mind

I see the stars up above so peaceful.
When I look at the world so freely,
I wonder whether, in the end,
What was meant to love, accept, or defeat.
They called everyone in sight,
Yet I was all alone in the mists of time,
Hidden and apart from excesses,
Shutting my mind,
Not sharing one thought
But knowing who and why,
Not clearing my name,
Not wanting to open your mind to newer themes.

Overwhelming Hearts

It's overwhelming to see you complain.
You made decisions without talking to me.
Yet my heart breaks
Because you watch, wait, and see
If I have made a mistake
While you have made the biggest mistake of all
By not accepting me or loving me,
Forgetting the best policy is acceptance of change.
What keeps you from knowing who I really am?
You're headstrong.
I'll live longer
Because I'm not always too serious and stressed out.
I'm sweet, kind, fun-loving, and smart.

Picture on the Wall

As I walked, expecting to see
This picture on the wall,
So soft, distinguished, ancient history,
Imposing soft, abnormal curves,
What was so distant and so clear?
As I felt emotional structure
When the structure of a Roman god
Measured the distance and the genders,
Or so I have heard, neither knew
This picture on the wall.
So much energy, animation, and togetherness
As I walk to discover the piece on the wall.

Poets' Expectations

Poets were expected to defend
As their minds, emotions, and kindness
Were heard and the words spoken
With the phrase of mind—
I am a poet!
The open desire to face remaining goals,
My status as a poet reflects my emotions
Determines my goals, as this is mine.
I write to complete.
You had me feeling sluggish to defend.
I see what is a reflection of me
As I see the glass mirror—
This is my signature of life,
As this is my expectation as a poet.

Pure Lust

Very little lust love appears
When there's reason to create such pure affection
With grace of hunger
To seal with a blind page
Written in a risk of night.
Only pronouns desire to move so quickly,
And that satisfies one's love,
But when there's another
That creates such termination,
There's no choice of one's heart
That will be broken into one's love.

Reach for a Carrie

As I glanced slowly as the emotions flared,
The darkness led into the affair
As he interrupted the depths of my love
Into his legendary mind.
I ran as far as I saw the darkness,
The pale blue figure standing
As I spread deep into an imagined touch and soul,
Rubbing his fingers deep into my hair.
As he reached for my lips
And released his kiss,
I heard a loud scream.
I felt intimidated, afraid,
Haunting mistress led into the midnight air
As I peeked through, into one's heart.

Realization

I once had a dream of running enemies
That opened the door and led me in.
Now I crown my sour lips in vain,
Using real anger and restructuring my sins.
I manipulate the pain with your wish,
Provoking the sound of hope and love
To cover up the demands of others.
I was unsure that love would not return
Because of the top officials. Human,
Untrustworthy to my kind,
Cursing and blaming human values
As if in a strange personal and social crisis.
Escaping all difficult memories left unsolved,
Now I'm not returning to your wish.

Remorse

I reminded you again about how I felt.
That never ended with a laugh.
But I revealed the remorse about whom—
Who left it behind my back?
Yet I return to trying to recover,
Releasing it out in the open.
My actions seen the vain you brought to life.
Now I remind you to live up to trying to do better,
Restoring the pain of innocents,
Not giving back but taking too much advantage,
Is to be true as I revealed my adventures!

Sabrina

I hear you sing in a venue;
I see you dance on, persisting.
You gave your heart to wonders
As where I see you touched your soul;
That touched me deeply.
I hear you say what seems to change
Your smile that lead the since of brave.
Now you have inspired me to touch my soul.
That freed you from the burning sun.
But the weather never changes.
I feel you here on kingdom come.
That seemed to lade perfection
Into the love that is worth the wait.
I can hear you say that seems to change
As I see you sitting on the land, traveling by train.

Since When

Since when did I feel for you?
You put me down and turn me blue.
You think love is all about beauty.
You have no respect or goodness.
But you feel above the clouds,
Cheering for the gods of all gods
And finding no return of your culture,
Winning for the balance of love
When all attractions and no return of mankind.

Singing a Different Tune

As I knelt and heard,
The voices among my destiny
leered, ravishing with each emotion.
But I will sing a different tune
As I ravish against my peers,
And I will maintain my soul
As I revive my love and perfection,
Only I can flourish the voices,
As the destiny is obscure,
And I will sing a different tune.

Someone Is Watching

There's someone who is watching
That I'm getting around
As if I'm going in circles.
I'm doing all the walking,
Paying more attention to myself,
Listening to others' echoes.
But I felt threatened as I felt closer to your lies,
Pointing, staring, watching,
Hearing and listening to my words
As I paid more attention to my surroundings
And listened to your echoes
As if I felt closer to your lies.

Sophisticate

You like to play saxophone
In the nearby night club.
I sit close to my window,
And I listen to jazz for hours
Before going to bed.
I never have enough.
When you are down on your luck,
You play how you feel.
Your affection for sophisticated sound
Left you a sustaining love for jazz
When you discovered what love
Was when you learned to say how you felt
And how to find it in your heart!
The saxophone discovers who you are.

Sound

Listen to this sound of the winds
As I whisper the words.
Listen to the sound of my feet,
The words of my soul
That travel far to create.
Soon there will be the fleet
Sound becoming a young woman
Whispering the sound for help;
Be on your silent bed.

Standards

I have standards that can secure my loneliness
For change, love, and consideration
To manage self-reliance and faith
While others couldn't afford me or care enough.
That's worth the acceptance of true love:
To honor my self-expressions
That you see the bad standards,
That you set for yourself,
That I couldn't learn anything about you,
And that you didn't want to learn about me.
I ask, "Where, why, and why not?"

Such Concerns and Such Liberation

The light came with a shadow
Facing her dreams and a mirror
As each glance forced her eyes to see
But a light put on a mantel.
Outburst of flames in such concerns,
The cruelties are discarded for others' positions
Only if you see appearing from such distance
Dreaming in such liberations
But to reach when the results,
When the results return to their own positions.

Surprise

I heard an enormous bang from afar;
I had no defense from the start.
But I opened my young eyes,
And I hummed my fears
As I soothingly rested above.
I sank my love and stretched my heart
That seemed to scatter my stumbling soul.
As I peered slowly frightened,
I kept a glance of previous surprise.
I shrugged, finding no harm.
I expected to see a river,
Sleek pool, and a crushing medal shimmered.
I returned with no defense from the start
As if I pointed quietly from afar.

The Ghost

The ghost is outside watching within,
And we're inside.
There's no running away
But to listen to you complain.
The tears are ready to fall
As the fears are close to install.
There's no giving up
But to feel the breeze that slows me down.
There's nothing to do but to feel strong.
As I hear the whispering soul,
It climbs the walls of a strange ghost.
I feel afraid, and nothing seems to break.
I watched the lines of a strange soul,
Looking over my shoulders.
When I spin around and run for miles,
There's no turning back, but slowly I discover
That I'm not alone!

The Harvest

I can smell the harvest
As I can deliver more consequences.
If you still love me,
I'll catch the heart of your
Consistency and faith,
And yet I endure the time I spend
With you.
I embrace the love around too
As I endure the moment when we are together
And we can carry on loving forever.

The Queen

In the world undiscovered
Was once a queen evil and vain.
Her human curse had been tossed away.
She dreamed her life ran far and wide,
As her memories had been replaced.
But faith covers the stranger's soul;
Her lover had swallowed his pride.
The crown was lost; it hadn't been found.
The dream had been told
That she unsolved the missing crown.
His name would be cursed.
The soul of the queen was uncured;
Who places her crown for the sound of gold?
And there she soon was frozen
As she took the spill,
And she turned into stone.

There's No Time . . .

Some will come to see
As I reach for the sky
There's no time to run away
When I'm reaching up high.
And I can't stop thinking,
Thinking about neglecting everyone
As I'm touching the sky
That I climb to obfuscate my time.
When it's close to my prime,
I reply and reserve as I touch the sky.

This Kind

There was something about you
That attracted my soul.
As I embrace the tenderness kind,
The greater heart, as I lay out my emotions
And speak for my kind,
I pledge to inspire love
And tolerance as I embrace your kind.

Timid

I felt timid that you didn't believe in me.
You felt I was unconfident and unreliable.
I felt that you had me convinced,
But I didn't buy the worst of you.
There are words and used morals,
But you are no better.
Now I am confident that you had what
Led me to believe
You had no timid values of truth.

Decline

I reveal the stubbornness prune
As the legendary rewinds
And everything declines,
As I reveal the stubbornness prune—
But I will remind the time
When I reveal the stubbornness prune
That can hear the one that will decline.

Insecure

I feel someone is near
Until someone tries humanity,
But no one will come to see.
Now I feel so insecure; no one knows how it feels
Being ignored or being harassed.
I will let you know how it feels:
As if you were to live in hysteria,
Outbreaks of uncontrolled madness
Or hatred, anxiety
Against humans or children.
I see that they are called bullies!

Untitled

How can you forgive if you were not forgiven?
By not listening to reasons
Or interacting with growth.
I discussed emotional needs,
By your disapproval, avoidance, and coldness!
Yet I am aware of such painless memories
That led me to return.
But you avoid such tremendous effort
Of loving me, comforting me, and closure.

Vivid Blackmail

I haven't been close.
I haven't been near.
So why are you using restrictions
And keeping me in fear?
You would like to see me use the law,
Using blackmail and all,
Damaging control of my dreams and extremes.
So why you are here, saying this thing about secret love
When there is no love to give and take?
Give me a break
And take a drink of fresh lemonade.

With or Without a Kiss

I remember when I was young
I thought that love came in all sizes and shapes—
Tall, short, big, or small,
Man, woman, or child.
Learning what had with confidence
That the word *advantage* means so much more,
One child said,
"If I give you a kiss,
I can be your friend."
I had been taken advantage of;
Still I couldn't have had a friend,
With or without a kiss,
If I had said yes.
He would have taken me for a ride,
Pretending I was just another person
Looking for adventure.
I'm still looking for a perfect friend.

Within Yourself

Who belongs in the line of fire?
As the fire's hard to blow within,
The liar lays the tire dust
And the skin deepens within
As if you seek the lust and the sins
Hearing the souls and the king's laughter
Thinking of yourself as heros.
Liar lies within the narrows and the lines of fire.
Reframing, the queen of sorrows sneers,
Remaining the lust of heros, fools' dust
As you were to say the fool is within yourself.

You Don't Know What I Want . . .

I have lived my life knowing what I wanted,
But every turn I made was left unopened
Because you had left me unhappy.
Gossip, mistrust, disloyalty, and underachievement
Are always in my dreams,
Because you don't know what I wanted.
Now you live not knowing.
I'll never give you that chance to get to know me.
Good night, bad memories.

You Don't Need to Know

I travel around the globe.
You don't need to know
Where I'm going.
The wind is taking me far—
As if you don't need to know,
Listening to calls that were my own personal zone,
Lingering into the night
As I find my way through in the blink of an eye.
Listening to the words of the singer
As they sang to the words.
What was my own—
As if you don't need to know
What was for me, where and when.
As if you think of yourself bigger than me,
Finding me and spying on me,
As if you don't need to know.

You're Not Happy

Why do you think that I'm not happy?
Yet I like to travel far
And yet you're not happy to see me.
You jump to conclusions
And land on the horizon.
But yet you're not happy to see me.
You begin to feel and to think I'm after you,
Later to lip and to
Lie about me.
But your luck has changed
Because you didn't listen.
There were times that months had gone by
And you didn't apologize.
I still find you mysteriously pretend to be in power.
But did you ever ask me all the right questions?
That seems like the reasons to referee the rules of one's life.
And you say secrets that you share to the world;
that seemed like I'm feeling small and worthless,
Putting me under the strangest thin line.
But here is the tip:
The next time, someone else had watched you,
Someone will find you fallen.
The day you fall
You don't have someone next to you
Walking a mile to be in your shoes!

About the Book

I reflected on my heart to find the right words to express my emotions and clearly get across with the vulnerable experience. I live to dream to create such concepts in my writing. I often see it through flowers in different colors that speak to me. I choose to climb the highest growth of my potential by seeing it in my pride. I try to be inspired and to confide in my work. I am often shared among my love ones. *Voices in the Garden* is my second book of poetry. And I will continue to write with many emotions and many colors that will inspire the horizons to come.

About the Author

Lucia Chiappara-Bennett enjoys creating poetry, watching movies, and listening to music. She was born in Montreal and raised in Ontario, Canada. She enjoys spending most of her time with her daughter, Sabrina, and her husband, Craig.